LIONEL MESSI

BY PAUL LOGOTHETIS

SportsZone

An Imprint of Abdo Publishing
abdopublishing.com

abdopublishing.com

Published by Abdo Publishing, a division of ABDO, PO Box 398166, Minneapolis, Minnesota 55439. Copyright © 2016 by Abdo Consulting Group, Inc. International copyrights reserved in all countries. No part of this book may be reproduced in any form without written permission from the publisher. SportsZone™ is a trademark and logo of Abdo Publishing.

Printed in the United States of America, North Mankato, Minnesota
042015
092015

Cover Photo: Jonas Ekstromer/Scanpix Sweden/AP Images
Interior Photos: Jonas Ekstromer/Scanpix Sweden/AP Images, 1; Alvaro Barrientos/AP Images, 4; Kyodo/AP Images, 7; Javier Barbancho/AP Images, 9; Manu Fernandez/AP Images, 11, 12, 25, 26; Bernat Amangue/AP Images, 15; Francesco Pecoraro/AP Images, 17; Victor R. Caivano/AP Images, 18; Luca Bruno/AP Images, 21; Julian Rojas/AP Images, 22; Nick Potts/Press Association/AP Images, 29

Editor: Nick Rebman
Series Designer: Craig Hinton

Library of Congress Control Number: 2015931752

Cataloging-in-Publication Data
Logothetis, Paul.
 Lionel Messi: Soccer sensation / Paul Logothetis.
   p. cm. -- (Playmakers)
Includes bibliographical references and index.
ISBN 978-1-62403-839-6
1. Messi, Lionel, 1987- --Juvenile literature. 2. Soccer players--Argentina--Biography--Juvenile literature.   I. Title.
796.334092--dc23
 [B]   2015931752

TABLE OF CONTENTS

Lionel Messi

CHAPTER 1

THE FLEA

Lionel Messi weaved his way through defenders. It looked like they were stick men. He started at the halfway line. He moved up the field past five players. All of the FC Barcelona fans rose to their feet. Something magical was happening. Messi then went around the keeper to score a remarkable goal.

Messi was only 19 years old. But he was already following in the footsteps of his hero,

Lionel Messi tries to control the ball at FC Barcelona's Camp Nou stadium.

Diego Maradona. Many believe Maradona scored the best goal ever. It happened at the 1986 World Cup. Messi's goal happened in 2007. It was nearly identical.

Just like Maradona, Messi was from Argentina. And like Maradona, he played professionally for Barcelona. But now Messi was making his own mark.

Messi is famous for wearing the No. 10 jersey at Barcelona. Messi wore No. 30 and No. 19 before No. 10 became available for him. Legends such as Ronaldo of Brazil and Diego Maradona wore the same No. 10 before Messi.

As a young boy, Lionel Messi's friends called him Leo. He had always been small. He earned his nickname, "The Flea," very early in life. Like a flea, Leo was small and pesky. His opponents could not stop him no matter how hard they tried.

Leo often practiced with a tennis ball. When he could not find one, he rolled up plastic bags or gym socks. Leo hated being without a ball.

Argentina coach Diego Maradona, *left*, speaks to Messi during a World Cup game in 2010.

Leo and his brothers spent a lot of time at their grandmother Celia's house. They ate pasta and then played soccer in the street. The games often ended with all three boys in a bad mood. No one in the family liked losing.

Leo was crazy about soccer. But he was small and shy. So he played with only his brothers. He finally got a chance to play with other kids when he was five years old. A local coach saw him playing with his tennis ball. The coach worried about Leo's small size. But Celia encouraged the coach to take a chance.

The coach invited Leo to play. Leo jumped on the ball and sped toward goal. His grandmother cheered him on.

Messi credits his grandmother with pushing his love for soccer. She used to go to all of his games. She passed away when he was 10. He celebrates every goal by pointing to the sky. He does this to honor his grandmother.

Like a flea, Leo kept overcoming bigger obstacles. He could dribble through defenses. He moved the ball with ease. It seemed the ball was tied to his foot with a string. Leo was easy to spot in team pictures. He was always the smallest boy. His uniform was much too big for him. But he was big enough to meet any challenge on the field.

Leo started playing for Newell's Old Boys when he was eight. Newell's is one of two teams in Leo's hometown of

Messi dribbles past an opponent in a 2005 game against Cádiz.

Rosario. Playing for them was a dream come true. Leo's whole family loved the club. The team improved right away when Leo arrived. They lost only one game in four years with Leo on the team.

But Leo's small body was holding him back. Doctors found a growth problem. Leo would need growth hormone injections to cure it. These injections had to happen every month for several years. But they would make a big difference in his career.

The injections were very expensive. Leo's family did not have enough money for them. Many people in Argentina could not find jobs at that time. The Messi family decided to leave the country. Leo's father wanted Leo to play in Europe. Europe had jobs and the world's best soccer teams.

Lionel Messi has a son named Thiago. He was born in 2012. Thiago became a member of Newell's Old Boys when he was only a baby. Thiago's mother is Antonella Roccuzzo. She is from Rosario, just like Lionel.

So the family traveled to Spain. They set up a tryout with FC Barcelona. Many fans call the team *Barca* for short. It is pronounced "Bar-suh."

Leo again amazed people with his skills. Barcelona's coach knew he had to sign Leo. He risked losing Leo to another team if he did not do it right away. But he could not find a piece of

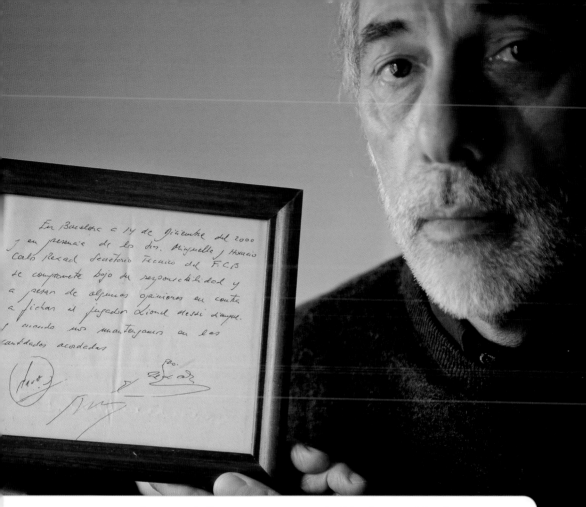

Horacio Gaggioli, a sports agent, holds the napkin that says Lionel Messi would play for Barcelona.

paper to write the contract. So he wrote it on a napkin. It said Leo would play for Barcelona. That napkin is famous now. It is kept in a safe.

At age 13, Leo moved to Barcelona with his family. He was ready to take the next step in his incredible career.

CHAPTER 2

LA MASIA

Moving to Europe gave Lionel Messi a great opportunity. He could play soccer with the best players in the world.

Leo was admitted to La Masia. That is the academy where Barcelona's young players go. They attend school during the day. In the afternoon they play soccer. Only the best players from around the world get in. Very few kids from South America make it. But Leo did.

Messi raises his arm in the air after scoring a goal against Osasuna in 2005.

"I've always been this way, ever since I was young. I've always really just liked soccer, and I've always devoted a lot of time to it. When I was a kid, my friends would call me to go out with them. But I would stay home because I had practice the next day." —Lionel Messi

Leo was now playing with other talented kids. This brought out the best in him. He learned a very important lesson after suffering an ankle injury. Leo loved to dribble the ball. But better opponents did not always allow him to dribble. They would tackle him hard. And they tackled him often.

Leo understood that he would have to change the way he played. He had good teammates, so he knew he could pass to them. Leo became a team player. This allowed him to get free in the field. If he got open he could receive passes from his teammates. And then he could score.

Leo was small and quiet. He often got tired. But with more training he got stronger. His growth injections also helped.

More people began to see how talented Leo was. Barca had teams at many different age levels. The coaches from each level wanted Leo to play for them. Leo made it all the way to Barcelona's top youth team. But he did not stay there long.

Messi celebrates a goal in a 2005 game against Albacete.

When he was only 16, Leo played his first game for Barcelona's top men's team. Barca was playing the best team in Portugal in an exhibition match. The other players were much more experienced than Leo. But he showed flashes of talent. Leo came on as a late substitute. He played for only 16 minutes. Even so, he nearly scored a goal.

Coaches could see Leo was nearly ready to play for Barca's top team. He needed only one more season with the younger players.

Messi's favorite food is called *milanesa*. It is breaded meat. It can also be served covered in ham and cheese. It usually comes with french fries. Messi loves to drink Coca-Cola with ice cream. But his coaches do not like him eating junk food. They want him to stay strong and healthy.

The 2004 season was about to begin. Barcelona's coach moved Leo to the first team. Leo was only 17. He would be playing in front of huge crowds. And he would be sharing the field with some amazing players. His teammates included Ronaldinho, Samuel Eto'o, and Andrés Iniesta. They were some of the best in the world.

Leo did not score in his first six games. But that changed in his seventh game. Ronaldinho lobbed a pass over the defense. Then Leo kicked the ball over the keeper to score. He jumped on Ronaldinho's shoulders to celebrate. All of his teammates were very happy for him. The 99,000 fans at Barcelona's stadium were happy, too.

Leo scored his first hat trick against Real Madrid. A hat trick is when a player scores three goals in one game. FC Barcelona and Real Madrid are the two best teams in Spain. They

Messi signs autographs for fans before a match in Italy in 2006.

are fierce rivals. So scoring three times against them was a big accomplishment.

Leo was playing with many superstars. But he stood out. People noticed him for his size and skill. Leo was building a reputation as one of the world's best players.

Lionel Messi

CHAPTER 3

BECOMING THE BEST

Lionel Messi was making a bigger impact with every game. But he had some troubles with injuries during his first few seasons. And Barcelona struggled without him. Messi's career changed for the better when Barcelona hired a new coach.

Pep Guardiola took over in 2008. Pep used to play for Barcelona. He was very smart. He knew that Messi would be the key to Barca's success. So Pep

Messi dribbles the ball in a game with Argentina's national team.

decided Messi would be the focus of Barca's attack. Pep told other players to pass the ball to Messi when they could. Messi would receive the ball more often near his opponent's goal. That meant he could take more shots.

National Basketball Association (NBA) star Kobe Bryant is a huge soccer fan. He especially likes Barcelona. When Bryant plays for Team USA, he wears No. 10 in honor of Messi.

Messi scored two more goals against Real Madrid in 2009. Barca won the game 6–2 and claimed the Spanish title. Pep had used Messi as a roving striker in that game. That meant Messi could move around the field. He could even drop back to get the ball instead of always staying up front. It was the perfect decision. Messi soon played that position in every game.

Barca later played Manchester United in the Champions League final. This game would determine the best club team in Europe. Messi was going to face Cristiano Ronaldo. Ronaldo

Messi holds up his shoe after scoring a goal in the Champions League final in 2009.

had helped Manchester United win the English league. Many people said Ronaldo was the world's best player.

Early in the game, Ronaldo kicked a low shot toward Barcelona's goal. The ball hit the post but did not go in. Barca took control after that. In the second half, Messi scored on a header. He jumped so high that his shoe came off. Messi was thrilled to score such an important goal. He even celebrated with the shoe.

Barcelona won six trophies that season. These trophies included league and cup championships. No team had ever won so many titles in one season.

Lionel Messi

CHAPTER 4

BEING THE BEST

Lionel Messi was only 22 when he won the Golden Ball. This trophy is given to the world's best player. Cristiano Ronaldo had won it the previous year. But now Messi was the best. In fact, he won the award for four straight years. No player had ever won it so many times in a row.

Messi was very important to Barca. So he signed a new contract in 2013. It said he would make more than $20 million a year.

Messi points to the sky after scoring a goal against Malaga in 2013.

Messi scored goal after goal. He was coming close to breaking many records. He scored four goals in a match against English club Arsenal. The Arsenal coach said watching Messi was like watching a video game. Messi scored 47 goals in 2010 as Barca won the Spanish title again.

In 2012 Messi scored an incredible 91 goals. He scored in Spanish league games. He scored in Champions League games. He scored in cup games and World Cup qualifiers. No player had ever scored so many goals in a year. The previous record was 85.

That same season, Cristiano Ronaldo had started playing for Real Madrid. Now the world's two best players were on rival teams. This pushed Messi to improve. Both Messi and Ronaldo wanted to be the best. The next season, they each scored 53 goals. But Messi was doing more than scoring goals. He also had 24 assists. Ronaldo had only 13.

Messi led Barca to another Champions League trophy. He even scored against Real Madrid in the semifinals. In the final,

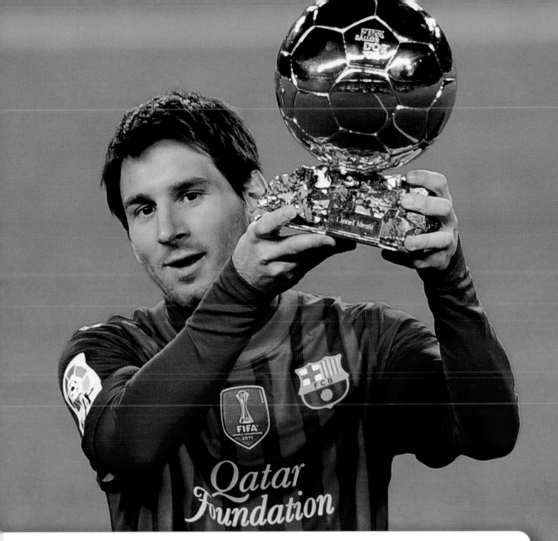

Messi holds up the Golden Ball trophy after winning the award for the third time.

Barca beat Manchester United again. This time it happened in London, England. With Messi in top form, FC Barcelona was proving difficult to beat.

CHAPTER 5

SETTING RECORDS

Lionel Messi seemed to score from every different angle. And he scored using many different kinds of shots. He could score with long-range shots. He could score up close. He could score with his left foot or his right.

In 2012 Messi showed these talents in the Champions League. He scored a record five goals in one game. It came as no surprise to people who knew Messi. Years earlier, he had scored five goals in a

Messi, *left*, competes for the ball against Valencia player Jonas.

game as a teenager. But this time it was against the best players in the world.

Opponents kept trying to stop Messi. But no one seemed to be able to. He kept setting records. In 2012 he became Barca's top scorer of all time with his 233rd goal. By the end of that season, he had scored a record 73 goals. In 2014 he broke the career record of 251 goals in the Spanish league. Messi helped Barcelona win 21 trophies in his first 10 seasons at Barca. He also helped Argentina win the Olympic soccer gold medal in 2008.

Messi wants to play his last season with Newell's Old Boys. Newell's is his favorite club in Argentina. His hero, Diego Maradona, also played there.

Everyone agrees that Messi is a great player. If he can win the World Cup, they might say he is the best ever. In 2014 Messi played very well in the tournament. Argentina reached the final game. But Messi could not score. Argentina lost 1–0 to

Messi hangs his head after Germany scored against Argentina in the World Cup final.

Germany. This left Messi without a championship in the world's biggest tournament.

It was a big disappointment for Messi. Even so, he is happy to be doing what he loves. And after scoring more than 400 goals, there seems to be no stopping him.

FUN FACTS AND QUOTES

- Messi is from Argentina, where Spanish is spoken. So his nickname, "The Flea," is *La Pulga* in Spanish.

- Messi is on course to become one of the greatest goal scorers in soccer history. Messi and Cristiano Ronaldo are both trying to set the record for most career goals scored in the Champions League. They have both passed Real Madrid striker Raúl González's record of 71.

- Argentina has a population of more than 40 million. It has produced some of the most exciting soccer players in history. They include Diego Maradona, Alfredo Di Stefano, Gabriel Batistuta, Mario Kempes, and Daniel Passarella.

- Messi never talks about himself even when scoring many goals in a game. He always thanks his teammates and focuses on the team's achievement.

- *"He does everything, and he does it every three days. He doesn't just score goals, he scores great goals; each one is better than the last. We are seeing the very best in action."* —Pep Guardiola

WEBSITES

To learn more about Playmakers, visit **booklinks.abdopublishing.com**. These links are routinely monitored and updated to provide the most current information available.

GLOSSARY

assist

A pass to a teammate that leads to goal.

contract

A written agreement between two or more people.

defender

A player whose position is in front of the keeper to help stop opponents from scoring.

dribble

A move that allows a player to control the ball and move it upfield.

header

Using one's head to guide the ball.

injection

A way of putting medicine in the body through a needle.

keeper

The player who defends the goal and can use his hands.

reputation

The opinion that other people have about a person.

striker

The team's best scorer, who plays more forward than everyone else. A roving striker moves around with more freedom in the attack.

substitute

A player who comes off the bench to replace another on the field.

tackle

To slide toward a player and try to get the ball away from him.

INDEX

FURTHER RESOURCES

Hoena, Blake. *Everything Soccer*. Washington, DC: National Geographic
    Society, 2014.

Hornby, Hugh. *Soccer*. New York: DK Publishing, 2010.

Jökulsson, Illugi. *Messi*. New York: Abbeville Kids, 2014.

Jökulsson, Illugi. *Stars of the World Cup*. New York: Abbeville Kids, 2014.